AIDE-MÉMOIRE

AIDE-MÉMOIRE

by

Ruth Roach Pierson

BuschekBooks
Ottawa

Library and Archives Canada Cataloguing in Publication

Pierson, Ruth Roach, 1938–
        Aide-mémoire / by Ruth Roach Pierson.

Poems.
Includes text in German.
ISBN 978-1-894543-43-9

        I. Title.

PS8581.I2815A74 2007   C811'.6   C2007-904022-5

Front cover photo by Lindy Smith.
Author photo by Sarah Hadley.

Printed in Canada by Hignell Book Printing, Winnipeg, Manitoba.

BuschekBooks
P.O. Box 74053
5 Beechwood Avenue
Ottawa, Ontario K1M 2H9
Canada

BuschekBooks gratefully acknowledges the support of the Canada Council
for the Arts for its publishing program.

 Conseil des Arts   Canada Council
du Canada   for the Arts

For my dear friend Thelma
and my beloved Aunt Louise

Table of Contents

I: Simultaneities

II: La Grande Illusion

III: A Little Life

IV: After the Flower Show

We lose everything, but make harvest
of the consequence it was to us. Memory
builds this kingdom from the fragments
and approximation. We are gleaners who fill
the barn for the winter that comes on.
Jack Gilbert, from "Moreover."

"Why is back the most beautiful direction?"
Anne Compton, *processional*

I

Simultaneities

THE MARROW

Another of those down-at-the-mouth January days. Even the cats are cross.
The Maine Coon pads across the carpet and sits, Sumo-like, splat
on top of the orange tabby. How gauche I was last night! In the garden,
a dull rain falls so slowly that drops collect on the underside of branches and hang
bud-like, upside-down and out of season. False tears

like the five small crystal spheres dripping from the woman's
mascaraed eyes in Man Ray's photograph. We see the world
through a mesh of likenesses, one hooking another,
until it's impossible to sever the linked hoops back
to recover the nub, the marrow of a thing.

Everything tends towards *aide-mémoire*—moaning doves,
a hotel window overlooking a courtyard in ruins, a clock
ticking, the airless still of mothballs and African violets. Opening a book
closed tight for years, I find your inscription, with its precise grace,
a reminder not all was lies and strife. Morning dissolves

into afternoon, the rain doesn't let up and I can't shake
my discontent with that self of the night before. How could
I so offend? No comfort in the thought I was in disguise,
a mawkish double, self-absorbed. If only
I could cast off that habit of mind, the self,

as in a blast of wind, the bare-limbed tree shudders free of rain.

Sadness exists, I read in a book,
but, not having the substance
of an instrument like an umbrella,
deflects no rain. If to have Being
requires doing, then rain, I reflect,
has Being, for rain can deflect

sadness. At least some rains will.
Verging-on-mist rain. Or soft volleys
on the roof like the ripple of mice running
between the floor of the apartment above
and the ceiling of the room where I sat writing,
at 3:00 a.m., the mice my only company,

an essay on fifteenth-century popular piety
taking untidy shape under my cramped
hand, clenched around the fountain pen
I wrote with then, when it was *de rigueur*
to write in ink and keep your longhand tools
in a Dundee marmalade jar. That kind

of rain. And this steady drizzle
like fingers hammering
on a dampered keyboard,
a rain that wraps me now
in its nostalgic cocoon.

But the sick child kept home from school
heard sadness in such hushed patter, a sadness
with as much Being as colouring books, radio soaps,
or the tray her mother brings to her bedside table,
bearing tapioca pudding and camomile tea.

SIMULTANEITIES

I'd forgotten the lesson
from *Last Year at Marienbad*
summed up in a *New Yorker* spoof:
The space-time
continuum in this hotel
is all screwed up. Space,

a geographer friend advised,
would solve your problem,
and I moved half a continent away.
There I waited for time,
as promised in the old saw,
to heal all wounds. Early

in the quattrocento, the Florentine
Masaccio mastered the melding
of time and space. Within a single frame
painted the beginning, middle
and end of Jesus' parable
about rendering unto Caesar. By mid-century

his Renaissance brethren in Flanders
had a ploy of their own: a perspective
at once telescopic and microscopic, every
castle turret in the distance as distinct
as every hair on the head

of the foregrounded Virgin. Nearing
our end we all receive such skills,
if skill is the word. Tendency, maybe.
In any case what's near and far meet
on the same plain, yesterday
and today collide on the same canvas,

and that old wound stings
as sharply as if I lived in the same house,
on the same street as then,
when I was young and listening
to Louis Armstrong's "What a Wonderful World."

VENTRILOQUISM

I couldn't stop acting the perky
spunky flibbertigibbet I imagine
you knew me as then   volumes
we could have spoken but
so risky   your hurt
at my forgetting the when
and where of our last encounter
my flashback to the scorch

of your disapproval—how
you compared my mind
to the chaos of my purse—
lipsticks car keys pencils
chewing gum no surprise
you still invest certain things
with special significance   so
I didn't confess I'd just bought
the Last Songs of Richard Strauss
on my way to our rendezvous—

at Jacques Omelettes—quiche
for both of us but not the same
white wine we settled
for a back and forth Being
authenticity Sebald
memory Plato's alleged
ventriloquism you
couldn't stop playing
the stern professor a tautness
straining your mouth my smile
hardening like polyurethane

EYES WIDE OPEN

As though I were in effigy, mummified scrap
of that girl you were gaga over and who
requited that infatuation. Again you lapse
into lecture—Santayana, Rome,
your quest for spirituality. Not one question
about the me between the student I was then
and the person I am now—forty years

of appetites cultivated, good friends
and bad, tardily learned lessons, ambitions filled
or foiled. Fairly folderol our Toronto meeting
last April. Now it's Victoria, rain-soaked and October.
Once again, I forget to ask
why, after four decades, you've tracked
me down. I could have stemmed
your stream of words by saying
Between desire and the given

yawns a chasm. Would you mind
removing your glasses, you ask.
Taken aback—my eyes no longer wide-eyed
and silky brown—I oblige and instantly
rue the act, so creepily like the starlet
lifting her skirt for the Hollywood mogul,
the courtesan disrobing under a man's

imperious gaze. Lashes, unfortunately,
shorten over time, and eyes, receding
into sockets, lose not only luster
but size. Peering, they acquire a pinched,
I could almost say a beady look.

A Distant Caw

You complained that I collect experiences
the way boys collect baseball cards.
And I did. Repose, an empty canvas
to be filled, still water to be stirred. Now, I savour
the snow's quiet falling, each flake isolate,
almost knowable. A great lake lies somewhere near
but not within walkable distance. The flakes
thicken as though layering wraps against the cold.
A crow's black flashes blacker against the lambent white,
a cardinal's red, more red. I hunger for greater
and greater stillness, for a blotting out of voices rising
from the floor below, sounds made by a shovel
scraping snow from the path.
                                        Enough
the distant caw breaking the white silence,
enough the blood-hum faint in my ears.

ARCHAEOLOGY

Knee-deep in knapsacks, a sidewalk café
packed with students kicking back, the air
filled with chatter and claptrap. At one table,
sitting upright, two greying teachers, resigned
and not a little jaded. In the dream I'm both
student and teacher, simultaneous selves
like geological strata, striations of a mountain.
Everybody a quarry, *Bildungsroman*. Not always

easy to accept the self of the amorphous now.
Easier the past selves for whom we feel
nostalgic or amazed. Sedimented selves
laid down in order but shifting, subject
to enfoldings, faults, reappearance.
Like the return every spring of robins
to the branches of the Persian lilac that spills
rufflike over my neighbour's fence.
Drowsy from its scent, I unearth

the girl packing her rucksack and heading off
with a class of German students and a borrowed
Fahrrad on a bicycle trip through the *Normandie*.
Her every sentence a venture onto the perilous
sandflats surrounding Mont St. Michel.
What she didn't see coming any more than those pilgrims

swallowed by the swift incoming Atlantic tide:
the teacher, ex-Nazi, turned on her,
and charged her, least articulate of the group,
with spreading ugly rumours about him and his wife.

Later he apologized, called it *unser schwarzer Tag*,
invited her home to sing around the piano
and play recorder with his family. This
insecure and sinister part of me I'd rather
keep buried. Past incarnations more truculent

than expected. And the girl:
recovered self, imprinted with shame.

Much, of course, was lost,
buried under moonscapes of rubble
after the blanket bombings.
Yet the family I spent
one year of high school with
had somehow salvaged china and silver,
sideboards, wardrobes,
an entire mahogany dining-room set.

> That first time
> they all stood at attention
> and shouted *Mahlzeit* in unison
> as *Vati* came through the door!

Ein Rätzel. How *die Spuren*
were thrown over so cleanly, so thoroughly.
Did they hold public bonfires?
Or were the vanishings enacted in isolated,
unspoken secrecy, survivors
gathered around the kitchen table,
tearing photos from the family album,
un-learning salutes and salutations,
devising and rehearsing narratives

of redemption? I arrived ten years
after the defeat. Not a button, not a scrap
of uniform nor shred of insignia. No books
on racial hygiene. And although every Volk
-respecting household once had one,
no *Mein Kampf.*

My first Christmas home, *Vati* sent me
Lebkuchen, echt Nürnberg Lebkuchen,
a crateful, the kind with chocolate on top,
Eucharist wafer on the bottom.

LEVELLING

When Adam delved and Eve span,
who was then a gentleman?★

The levelling chant repeats
like a reminiscence in her head that won't
dispel. A bell tolling: level, level,

level with me. She not sure she's reached
or sunk below her true level, and herself,
if sized up by an Auntie Mame, not

top drawer. Her father kept a spirit level
in his workbench drawer, a ruler-like tool
with a convex window on one side
into whose centre a bubble of air
floated when the instrument lay
in perfect accord with gravity and a

hypothetical horizon. A student of history,
she's always sided with the levellers,
that alluring mix of hope and despair.
She regrets misplacing her father's device,
wishes she had it to lay on her breast and test
the evenness of her breath,
and if and how she might rebuild

her levelled spirit, levelled now in that
particular twentieth-century sense
of razed, *der Erde gleich gemacht*,
as a German soldier would have said of what
the *Wehrmacht* did in '43 to the Warsaw ghetto, then
to the whole city of Warsaw
while the Soviet army halted its advance
and waited on the banks of the Vistula

for the levelling to be done.

★*Chant from the 1381 Peasants' Revolt in England*

Crumpling in the heat, she watches beads of sweat
drop—pause—drop from the iron radiator.
Red, green and yellow peppers gutted
of membrane and flat, misshapen seeds,
lie on a cutting board beside mushrooms, pale
as flu-sick children, waiting to be destemmed.
                    Before she writes, to post
on her front door, *please leave behind the screen,*
she checks the dictionary for how to spell
courier—coureurs de bois. Or de ville? Curiouser
and curiouser. Courage, Sir.
                Recently she re-read Castiglione's
last *Book of the Courtier,* troubled
by its ending: daylight's first strands
threading in through the clefts in the shutters,
and Pietro Bembo's verdict on women—
suitable, or too carnal, for platonic love?—
deferred forever to the evening of that day.
             Back in the kitchen she's careful not
to cut herself on the charcuterie knife, abruptly
remembers studying *Fräulein von Scuterie*
in that seminar from the professor
who killed himself. They were never told how,
and she's forgotten his name, but not his lectures
on the German Romantics, those meanderings
by moonlight through dense cedar, loose
ends of memory scattered on a forest floor.
             Reluctantly she glances
at the morning paper spread upon the table,
cartoons and carnage cheek by jowl.

RAILWAY SIDING

Riding the down escalator,
I think I recognize the woman ahead,
ask if we know one another,
if she ever did Tai Chi. Yes,
she nods, for a few months, a few years ago.
For self-confidence, she adds, anxiety
flickering beneath the surface of her eyes.
I see that quiver often now
in the eyes of older women. The fear this world
would discard us if it could. Does,
sometimes, shunts our kind
onto an *Abstellgleis*, as the Germans
would say, a railway siding. We suspect
the world is right, we have nothing
more to offer, like a store cleaned out
in a fire sale, a looting. And frailty,
its metastasizing stealth, a stalker
on tiptoe. Every body part,
every brain cell, ambushed. Less,
we learn, is simply less.

JIM DINE IN LUDWIGSBURG

With an argot of finger-splayed hands
and valentine hearts in the shape
of two voluptuous curves
tapering to a single
point Jim Dine
spurted to the top of New York's art charts.

It was the 1960s,
the colours psychedelic.

He chose a bathrobe
to symbolize self, sleeves and torso
empty but columnar as though enclosing
an invisible man with a puffed-out chest
and a taste for garish opulence, pot
and pipe dreams,
love-ins.

But, of course, he's moved on.
No more hammers in jaunty conga line
bounding through the landscape.

It's 1994, and in Ludwigsburg,
Dine has only six days to fill
the *Kunstverein* walls. On the seventh,
a reception.   Fierce

his decisive first strokes, *the line from heart
to hand*, he says, masked
against dust and fumes, *stronger than ever.* Then he moves
in for the rub and scumble,
steps back, squints,
reaches for his eraser, a bread chunk
stuck to the end of a pole. Rough

and porous, the white-washed walls
resist as he struggles to charcoal icons,
larger-than-life, apotheosized, totemic—
the language now his own head,
gigantic; massive raven; towering owl.
Skull.   The final figure a tree

thrusting from the ground,
winter-naked, sparse limbs
thwarted in their reach, the whole
unspeakably stark. Defeated
and defiant.
                              Afterwards,

show over. Dine gone. Men in overalls
with rollers on poles rolling thick coats
of white over the eyes of the owl,
the raven's beak, the artist's brow-
knitted face, every last stroke

painted out.

You, too, Anna, knew white nights flecked with poplar kapok,
mosquitoes. But this is no longer the city of your stern age.
Soldier amputees beg in the streets. Babushkas, bent
and greying, before the Church on Spilt Blood.
But no frozen corpses or sated rats.

A few kopeks buys brown bread and a shot of vodka.
And though queues spring up in grocery stores, at ticket booths,
no lines of women huddle day after day outside Kresty prison.

Before the Russian Museum a busker belts "Your daddy's
reech, and your mama's good luckin'."
        Unaltered
the domes and spires glistening in the evening sun. Likewise
the Neva's tempered flow. But the rock bands on Palace Square,
the women in skimpy T-shirts and flirty high heels
tripping along Nevsky Prospect—they're new.

Amid a courtyard's roses and tall maples, a monument,
Modigliani svelte, obdurate. Your battered valise waits
in a hallway of the house on Fontanka. Hanging nearby
a lover's greatcoat, khaki, threadbare. Through thrown-
open windows foreign students hear Arkadii read

of unstable meanings. Above the resurrected Stray Dog,
a costly shop sells amber jewelry. Irrefutable you once wrote,
Anna, poet and prophet, Anna of all the Russians, today
I walked under the lyre-hung branches of Tsarskoye Selo.

MEMORY WORK

Resonant the river's changing
        name as it widens and flows
                east—Danube, Donau,

                Duna. Grander,
        less tumultuous than this
city's course. Berlin's boulevards

and streets have endured namings,
        unnamings and renamings more times
                than remembered. Underbedding every Um-

                benennung, a bloody Umwälzung
        or bloodless bouleversement. Clara-Zetkin-Straße
re-christened Dorotheenstraße, a Hohenzollern

Prinzessin preferred, after the wall's fall,
        to a militant Kommunistin. In the suburb
                Lichterfelde West, a cluster of barracks,

                formerly home to SS
        Leibstandarte Adolf Hitler. Earlier
a high school, before that

a military academy. And now
        the Bundesarchiv. Set into the sidewalk,
                before certain houses, Stolpersteine,

                cobblestones of worn brass,
        each engraved with a German Jew's
name and date of deportation, place

and year of death. All day in Berlin's Kreuzberg
        buses disgorge throngs before the Jewish,
                not the German Jewish, Museum. Elsewhere,

                afternoon crowds gather in Café Einstein, evenings
        in Restaurant Lubitsch. And yesterday, in the Neue
Nationale Galerie, a reading of the poems of Paul Celan.

II

La Grande Illusion

GADFLY

Audrey advises me my pituitary gland
needs work. A reflexologist, she can tell

from the soles of my feet.
But I confuse pituitary with pineal, the Cartesian

seat of the soul, the unpaired eye, the pineapple
of the brain. Carlyle's purse of the Body Social.

Would that I could experience a Pentecost or beckon
a Pegasus to remove with a blow of its hoof

all impediments. Meanwhile, I continue my search
for a pair of those duck-billed platypus shoes

I stomped around New Haven in when I wished
I could don a slinky Myrna Loy peignoir

and sit and listen to Puccini while performing
my morning *toilette*. But then I realize Audrey really means

pituitary gland, the small bi-lobed body at the base
of the brain, surgical removal of which

in monkeys stops the œstrous cycle, œstrous
being Greek for gadfly, breeze, and also sting,

as in something that goads one
to vehement appetite, passion, frenzy.

A Foreign Tongue

Hands plunge into suds and suddenly
there's Sara's bucket of knickers soaking
in the bath, Colleen mooching tickets
to flicks and cadging drinks and fags,
and the dingy flat we mismatched three
shared somewhere in WC2, a snazzy address
for impecunious students.
                        Four years
since I'd seen my hirsute bartender
from Birmingham, each of us now hitched
to somebody else. And over that whiter-shade-
of-pale summer, we two eked out our love's
dregs sloping off into church crypts,
ostensibly visited for their architecture,
and trading aching looks over foaming pints
of bitter in dozens of different pubs.
                    So what right have I,
now, to gasp over memoirs
and biographies, aghast
at the binges, the breakdowns,
the messy adulteries.
                       The past
is another country, someone once said.
And the past self, it seems, a stranger
who spoke a foreign tongue. Back
                 at the sink, rinsing
the clothes I've washed by hand,
squeezing and twisting, I try to recall
the vernacular of that nimble-footed self:
lust in escrow, mind
less aware of double-dealing
than of feeling divided.
                   A London morning,
she steps out, dressed in Mary Quant,
onto Marylebone Road, heads for the British
Museum, pops into a caf for the *Guardian*, tea
and a slice, already dreaming of that evening's
chances of catching the glance of his hand
as he helps her off with her coat, strikes
a strike-anywhere match to light
her filtered Player's No. 6.

SODA POP SISTERS OF THE SOCK HOP

Our laughter fizzes like ice cream
dropped into root beer
as we remember
Rosenbloom emblem jackets,
cashmere sweater sets from Best's,
our first Maidenform bras.

No laughing matter, then,
what we wore—Evan Picone
pencil-straight skirts down to ankles
snug in angora bobby sox,
soap and water saddle shoes
we saddle soaped.

One slumber party, eight of us
(heads tiaraed in pin curls and spoolies)
shared a single lit cigarette.
Before that our major sin was stealing
cheap packets of hair dye
from the Five & Dime. Summers

we lazed lakeside at Aunt Louise's,
listening, in our Rose-Marie Reid swimsuits,
to Patti Page on K J R,
our during-the-school-year boyfriends
gone to Alaska for jobs on the boats
and the sex we Rhine maidens
and earth angels shrewdly withheld.

So here's to us: Nancy,
Grace, Liz and Barb,
Donna, two Carols, Ruth and Ann—
widows, divorcées, retirees. Oh,
to dance again, shoeless, the Swing
wag-hip and flirty, the Avalon
slow and close.

WHITE LIGHT AS BOTTLED PRESERVE

Last night, a pre-dawn storm.
Thunder. Jagged elbows of light.
Brassy, irreverent. Now
the aftermath light of this early morning—scoured
by the brillo pad of the storm—falls
on bedpost, floorboard, china bowl, each thing becoming
the thing it is, only more so. Tatter of ladybug husks
bejewelling the carpet, doilied table, chest of drawers.
        Transfiguring as a prism. More intense
than lantern flame. And more lasting. At least as long
as the purple cherries and fleshy halves of apricot and pear
stored once on pantry shelves. They shone.
I want to capture a handful of this light,
keep it with me in a sealed jar. Mason. Bell.
Longer than the firefly my mother bottled in West Virginia,
perforating the lid to bring it home to her daughter
stowed with grandparents in Seattle.

BURLAP COAT WITH A RED VELVET LINING

(After Luci Dilkus' "the Old Bag series")

shifting uneasily from foot to foot
you see the sag of your skin
in the burlap coat the artist has draped
over a hanger dangling from the ceiling

the jute, coarsely woven
basted with makeshift stitches
is crude cover for the velvet lining
a fire banked yet ardent

hummingbird-feeder red
glimmers at the end of each sleeve
and at the gaping, buttonless
unhemmed front

fraying thread
pooling at your feet

and you had almost forgotten…
the young woman modelling before the mirror
her mother kneeling on the floor
measuring to mark a full skirt's

hem, the job of daughter to turn
stand still, and, holding the pins, turn again
but you loosen your grasp and they spill
rattling into a disordered heap

and your mother's shrill *Why can't you learn
to organize your life!* and you look down
at your moving feet but can't stop
their shifting

GLASS EQUUS: ELEGY

atop my glass coffee table
a crystal horse flanked by frosted
Lalique stalagmites   each bearing
one red candle   fragile

as my lost friend Jeannie
Lespérance   her hopeful surname
lifted from a marriage of
brief duration   we'd escape

on steamy August late afternoons
numberless numbing hours
in the archives   hit an air-conditioned
Ottawa bar   ship out on a sea
of campari and soda   weaving
through archipelagos of Jeannie

whimsy   brittle
but brilliant   snappy volleys
of repartee from Lubitsch
and Capra films   whole plots
of Iris Murdoch novels recapped
every character's name

perfectly recalled   her scatty
quicksilver mind   colt-skittsh   balked
by rules   time-tables   bureaucratic
minutiae   that future in-
escapable

she'd one day escape   I always hoped
into an elsewhere   less censorious
more amenable to flights
of equine fantasy   somewhere   say
where crystal horses canter and capriole
like this one   a Jeannie gift   from years ago

As I walk this swath of land jutting
into the Pacific, its balance swung between wind
and water, outcrop and scarp, something unbidden,
maybe the light or the place itself,
sweeps my mind back to a high bluff
looking over the Atlantic. Promontories,
both, but this blunter point, dotted
with meadowfoam and weather-pocked stone formations,
once served as holding ground for bones
awaiting transport to the Middle Kingdom.

Young, we paid no heed to death or alignment
as we lay on that other headland, hidden
behind hummocks of wild blueberry. Tongues
twisting in illicit kisses, our fingers
plucked clusters of the tiny fruit
taut inside misted-blue skin. Hiss of surf
and a profuse wind, the only sounds.

Today both you and the husband I betrayed
are dead. The waves break here, as there,
against a shore's glacial erratics, salting
the light, as then, with upswept shards of sea.

THE UNCLENCHING

I've returned to where the husband
I had once is revered. The town
a paperweight of clouded-glass,
colander-domed. His portrait hangs,
framed, in the university library.

      I traipse the crooked streets
      heuristically, more sleuth,
      I tell myself, than tourist,
      climb the steep rise from the harbour,
      the hill barnacled with Paul Klee houses
      like children's wooden blocks brightly

coloured and askew, but braced
against gale-driven rains and snows
and the ropes of fog that spool in
from the sea over Cape Spear
and through the Narrows. Carew Street,

      Monkstown Road,

Prescott. My hooded
self, body clenched,
lurches into the blizzard's fury
toward the clapboard dwelling,
plaqued and painted green,
of my onetime husband's
widow.

      She offers peppermint tea. And photos,
      dusty, discoloured. I sip
      and smile, stay longer than expected, and afterwards
      regret not having asked if he'd still liked
      heist movies, the Meerschaum pipe
      we bought together in London,
      John Berryman poems.

By nightfall the wind has quieted,
and stars shine through pinholes
in the cleansed curve of the sky,
a few cloud wisps loitering
past the white of the moon.

SKYLINE

Like mercury rising, an elevator
climbs the unclad façade, while a crane's
pulley, on the makeshift roof,
reels up a crate. I watch,

rapt, until a flycatcher, slicing
my line of sight, lands on a nearby tree,
leaves emblazoned like shields
of hammered brass. A gust

of wind and my gaze turns
inward to that morning a lifetime ago
when I sat reading *I and Thou*,
immersed in the otherness

of cherry trees blossoming on the quad.
Till a passing couple, absorbed
in one another, caught my eye. Reaching
up, the man tugged on a branch,

and the scene's bright facets tumbled
apart, shattering to re-unite
in a different figuration. As a city's skyline
collapses, levels, and surges again.

Or a life's.
Though the order's otherwise.

THINKING OF A FORMER STUDENT IN EARLY AUTUMN

In this moment of grace—
the linden barely limned in yellow,
only a fraction of the maple rust-tipped—
to say *hold on, rescue's*
on the way
                 would be to lie,
as we lied to you then
who lay frail against pillows,
wasted from within by cells run
amok, charting your future: the thesis
you would write, the estranged
husband you would reconcile with,
the young daughter you would raise.
Nodding, we sought to hide
our disbelief and returned your smile
with ones we plagiarized and printed
on masked faces, our eyes
tears in the façade.

HIATUS

A pair high on that building's façade. *See,*
I start to say, but the word
doesn't come and the moment
passes, and you and I and our conversation

move on. That delay, like waiting
for a discontinued train or tulips to sprout
from squirreled-away bulbs. Synaptic
lapse or rogue virus in the mind's

search engine. One night I ransacked
my brain—Melanchton, Mitterand, Mirabeau
—but came up blank, the master diplomat,
architect of the Congress of Vienna eluding

the history teacher of so many years.
Same another night with the author of *Waiting*
for Godot (though I was once a fervent
theatre-goer). Fulfillment of Holmes'

furniture warehouse theory? Pack
the storage facility full, and for every new
Voltaire armchair or Kidderminster carpet,
an old one has to go. Or is utility, not space,

the principle? They carry limited
conversational cachet, yes, but the sculpted women
of Greek antiquity were more than merely
decorative, their heads bearing the weight

of entire entablatures. What determines
which facts are sent packing, which
granted permanent residence? Psychology, I'm sure,
has an answer. But its architraves escape me.

BLOOD ORANGES ON SIENA'S VIA DEL PARIDISO

Tired, I trudge from church to church,
museo to *museo*, a taste of citrus
on my tongue. Torqued bodies. Red
spurting from a gashed side. Corpse
lifted down from the cross like a flag
lowered from a mast. Sweet faced virgins,
too, of course, Pintoricchio's, Perugino's.
But everywhere mangled flesh and

martyrdom eclipse the peacock's
promise of eternal life. In Spello a gridiron
on which San Lorenzo roasted to death.
Here St. Catherine's severed head, broken-
toothed, eye-slits stitched shut. No vanishing point
for St. Sebastian pierced with arrows
or the defiled Iraqi prisoners pictured
in today's press. Duomo frescoes

honour Aeneas Sylvius Piccolomini,
his family crest five crescent moons
on a cross. Crowned Pius II,
he reigned a mere three years,
poisoned, some suspect, by disaffected
crusaders. He had, like many a pope,
called war against the infidel
holy. But please, not the saint who once stood

naked on Assisi's Piazza del Comune
proclaiming God's love—to all, surely,
sans frontières. San Francesco,
tell me the guidebook lies,
you sweet-tempered, grey-robed friar,
you poet-saint immortalized—*Brother Sun,
Sister Moon*—for preaching
to the birds.

But nothing tender in the down-
turned corners of her mouth, the severe
downward gaze of her eyes.
Imperious, this Madonna
della Misericordia,
        and
            unbending. Patroness
of executioners (note on her right
the black-hooded man), she towers
over her kneeling supplicants, commanding—
what? What bargain has she struck
with her devotees, what abasement
exacted in return for absolution
under her outstretched cape?
            No mere exercise in volume
or perspective, this early painting of Piero's
impastoed with lessons learned as child
or young man.
            Who was the dominatrix?

Mother?   Older sister?   Guild master's wife?

He's left no self-portrait among the canopied.
But down in the predella, a panel depicts two men
flagellating Christ.

In my mind's eye, a *carambolage*
of images, though it's years since you and I
saw Jean Gabin play the common soldier,
wounded, running with a *confrère*
over open land, the striven-for-border
buried under layers of ice-crusted snow.
With each step, the two sink, thigh-deep,
but struggle on, like a span of oxen
slogging through mire.

> A matter of preference:
> the cavalier French officer
> piping a tune on his fife while he executes
> a diversionary dance over the prison's
> parapets or the monocled precision
> of von Stroheim pulling white gloves
> over seared hands before bowing his body,
> braced from waist to chin, then snapping it
> back to toss down a schnapps.

Cataracts on the mind. So many.
All vying for the rank of grand. Honour,
as in military code of. Faith
in a cause worth dying for. On good days,
I incline towards love, the mirage
we once pursued. Leaning over tables
spread with maps, generals on both sides,
four- and five-starred, plot a war.
Did they truly think it would be fought
by gentlemen playing by *La Règle
du jeu?*

File back up the aisle of the cinema, walk
out into the street, preferably alone, the sheen
of neon streaking rain-wet asphalt. Post-war Prague.
Or is it Vienna, Warsaw, New York? Enter
a café or bar, clasp a mug in your hands, cold
meeting heat and the silk of liquid. Window-mirrored,
sleek shark-bellied cars flash by, every third the carrier
of a possible assassin. The echo of footsteps in the fog,
trench coats belted with cynicism. A flute's atonal notes
reverberate beneath your feet, other feet running fast
through criss-crossing chambers, tunnels, a subterranean
maze. A match is struck, and for a moment a single eye
peers out of the darkness, a look lucent with fear. Hunch-shouldered,
you shrug back into your coat, body hot, blood-heavy,
alive.

That old Andy Warhol trick with the split-screen,
except his screens were sometimes split six ways.
I can't remember how many frames it took to show
the hedonistic Adonis naked to the waist go on
and on about the feel of his long blond locks
brushing the nape of his neck. What is it with movies
you never forget, that draw you in and are more
than spectacle? Afterwards, walking out, you are young
and beautiful and enmeshed in a tragic love
with someone young and beautiful who wants you,
but oceans, accidents, marriages have come between,
so there's only this one long stolen night
in a hotel room, of course, neither posh
nor shabby. And you talk and talk
and eventually make love as you once did in a golden past
when you were both younger and even more beautiful.
And there's nothing for it but yet more talk and deep kisses
and a shower and a message on the hotel room phone
and your cell phones getting mixed up. And then
shortly after dawn, a taxi ride for you to Kennedy
(it turns out you've been in NYC all along) and for him,
the split now final, a short ride across town
to a breakfast date with one of the betrayed.

III

A Little Life

A Little Life

My tongue trips, commits
a fricative slip. *Convection,*
Dwight corrects, as I continue to say
confection for the fan that circulates
an even heat around meat loaf, soufflé,
peach and apple crumble. Or would,
if I could be bothered to bake.
Then my day takes a sharp
turn
                              and collides
with what the TTC would have us
not know: a jumper, the subway train
losing power at Ossington. Shaken,
the driver conducts us to the lead car's
one open door, the stranded in stasis
or milling on the platform.
                              Stomping off,
one indignant woman shouts:
You're morons to stop and gawk.
You should leave and get on
with your lives. Affronted
a young man explodes:
It's not every day you get to see
a dead body.
                              A teenager,
the crisis counselor in my cab
confides, someone with the whole
phantasmagoria of life left to live,
but who lacked
the conviction.
        At home I finally turn
the convection oven on. Resolved
to bake, not something sweet,
but hearty, nourishing, a dish to stick
to our ribs, my mother's nostrum,
or to keep body and soul together,

in the phrase of my friend and colleague
David, who died at forty, of melanoma,
leaving how many unwritten volumes
on the history of the Atlantic fishery.
And wife and ten-year-old son. David,
who took my hand in what was left of his
only days before dying and, pressing faintly,
whispered: *Live a little life for me.*

They'll never suffer from logorrhoea,
those men born on Kansas farms,
who name hunting dogs after sweethearts,
sisters-in-law, wives, moms.
Shirley, a favourite, rode behind Dwight
on the tractor's seat when he ploughed,
a rock between her jaws in wait
for when the boys had time to throw.
Grown, they shy away from affection
openly shown, only at ease
giving vent to the welling unspoken
over farm beasts and wild, injured things.
As when Frank, with a doll's bottle, nursed
a newborn skunk found lying, eyes unopened, in a field.

FARM WIFE, WESTERN QUEBEC, 1940

Malak, plying the back roads
in search of country folk,
has leapt from his jalopy and asked
her to pose. But she refuses
to smile. Spine strained back,
eyes locked against the sun,
she rises above the camera,
a sapling against the sky.

From under a man's worn cap,
its tweed bill twisted to the side,
her hair, all marcelling spent, hangs
in slack waves around a face grim
with impatience at this uncustomary
standing still. She wears, not trousers,

but a dress, its sleeves deflated,
paisley pattern sun-effaced,
a rent at the waist and an isosceles tear
below the bodice's last button. Meagre
sheath for a body sharp as a ploughshare
and gaunt. See the jut of hipbones
and the ache of veins tunnelled
beneath her arms' bare skin.

She grips the handles of the plough.

BETWEEN OUR HOUSES

Blue undiluted by cloud, sun
temperate, air pollution-free—
the only flaw the rasp
of broom on asphalt.
In that grim purpose she dons
for work in the garden where
I see her planting and weeding,
Catherine, our neighbour, stranger
to repose, is sweeping the drive
between our houses. Her broom's *scritch*

scritch intrudes on my indolence, interrupts
my musing on the goldfish, their languid
glissandos in the pond below the shedding
linden. It's not a day for thinking
about this dour neighbour, our adjacent lots
too often a battle zone. Catherine,
for whom Christ is the light of the world,
sees in trees only mess and obstructed
sunlight. She once felled three mulberries
along the fence, Dwight and I out of town
for his father's funeral. I try to forget

how I shouted at her, a sad, driven woman,
sadder now her husband has died. No,
on this rare almost perfect summer day
I want only moments like this morning's
when Dwight and I heard before we saw
a yellow oriole trilling, then its arcing flight
from the weeping purple beech
to the peak of the oak.

Rods, say,
not bundled
but singular as in spare
and spoil the child.
A switch grabbed by a father
to scare into breath a willful
two- or three-year-old
blue in the face. Staff,
maybe not, but rod
closer to correction,
chastisement
than to comfort. A steel bar
to strengthen a young
Kaiser's arm stiffened
his military resolve. Keith,
a friend, died despite
the metal halo screwed
into his head and to a rod
run down his spine. Hot rod,
fishing rod, divining rod. The hard-
bitten Philip Marlowe,
Sam Spade, Easy Rawlins
all packed
a rod. Golden or graphite,
wooden or bone, ramrod
or vertebral. The disciplined
child: did it learn to stand
upright, show backbone,
be a rock, solid,
unbiddable?

"Hand-me-downs"

a woman, baby strapped to her chest,
explains to her foreign helper, one hand
gesturing toward herself, the other
downward, the au pair mystified.
Complicated. So much is handed

down—beliefs, tastes, walking canes,
enmities. But we save the first-person phrase
for discarded clothes or maybe the odd
piece of furniture, bric-a-brac. Dwight's
birthday gift, when a boy, was a bike

handed down from his older brother,
Bob, who got the new one. Another year
the same story with a fishing rod. Quaint
that straitened past and its ways. We still
bequeath, of course, to the living

from the dead—Great Aunt Ethel's
golden slippers. Grandmother Martha's
hand-painted china. Uncle Nate's bone-
handled hunting knife. Handed down,
yes, but unencumbered by the weight

of that self-reflexive "me," its taint
of glad-handing charity, smug
funk the needy combing the aisles
of their local Goodwill can't help
but catch a whiff of.

Splitting Wedge

Heat from the sun coaxes
a whiff of cedar from the splintered wood.
Padlock sprung, the shed door
creaks open

and I step through into the grimy,
dust-covered dimness of the left-
behind. I tug on a cord
still dangling from the single-unshaded bulb,

the man from Snoqualmie Antiques
on my heels. A stash of tools greets us—rake, pitchfork,
pruning shears, shovel—rough-hewn handles
stooked in a corner. A rusting cross-cut

saw hangs from nails my dad
hammered into an exposed stud.
In shadows, the chimera of the rat my grand-dad
trapped and I, thrilled, ran with into the cabin

to scare my elders. The dealer spies
a pair of andirons barely visible
under a block and tackle's loosely coiled rope.
He'll take them plus the b & t, two hammers,

one monkey wrench, the double-bladed axe,
and the bow saw curved like one end of a cradle.
But not the splitting wedge
I will need for the task

of severing myself from this haven my forbears
named *Kwitcherbellyakin*, this spot unspoilt
except by time, this place on the banks
of a river little more than a stream.

No Right of Entry

It belongs to strangers now,
so I have no right to enter
and am, in this dream,
seeing it only from the outside
as I stand inside my grandparents'
old place, floorboards rotting,
roof collapsing, clapboard
straining loose from rusted nails.

I set out to circle
my parents' cabin,
make my way through fern
and unmowed grass
toward the stone steps
to the river. There I find
a bed of nursery flowers
planted in dry sand

where there should be wild sweet pea
and a tangle of blackberry brambles
and a bush we loved as children
because its leaves, when we held them
under water, shone
as though dipped in liquid mercury.

ENDINGS

From the last car of a train long as a vendetta,
frock-coated men and corseted women
bid farewell to a departing century,
white chambray fluttering dove-like
in raised hands waving.

Alone at the end, my father
found lurking confused on the stairs
to the basement of the Volunteer Park Museum,
sheepish as a three-year-old runaway
too far from home.

Queue after queue—before the bank
teller's window, slot machine, polling booth—
a ribbon unwinding down the block
and I at the frazzled end, fresh
out of lucre, luck, faith in the franchise,

like a square bracket stranded
at the end of a line, a derailed
man strapped to a stretcher in ER,
sucker punched, blood draining from his cheek,
balking at every query about next of kin.

The Cemetery on Old Topsail Road

An irreversible falling out
with his father was one rumour.
Boredom with life, others speculated,
or a disappointment with self deeper
than despair. What makes any of us
self-destruct?
                After dinner
we had walked to the small cemetery
at the head of Old Topsail Road,
where we danced over graves, drunk
on Christmas and the whirling snow,
but not over his grave, not yet dug.
                Word of his death came
later that day, slipped like an icicle
between my breasts, my unkind remarks
somehow more at fault than his hard,
persistent drinking—persistence
so greatly admired within the walls
of academe.
            I reassure myself,
he was already dead when we traipsed
between the headstones, tripped woozily
over the engraved slabs, heavy
with second helpings of turkey,
extra dollops of hard sauce on the dark
and steaming Christmas pudding.
Who knows the deep-down, the root,
the buried cause?
            Though a colleague,
I hardly knew him, liked him less,
couldn't see through his bumptious
bravado. It's more than thirty years now
and why this particular death haunts
is anyone's guess.
            Mine: the shock of it,
the awful marriage of frivolity and gravitas,
that variance at the heart of life
I've never learned, will never learn
to live with.

SNOW

Over night and on into morning, snow.
Dandruff-fine, light as dandelion fluff,
but persistent, accumulating, like gossip
about the man across the street, his fling
with the au pair from the old country,
everyone in the neighbourhood siding with the wife,
she who planned and planted the front garden,
trained purple clematis up the veranda trellis,
placed at the centre of the garden's orbit that
neo-Renaissance Madonna bought in an Orvieto *botteghe*
the summer back in Umbria with her parents.

Never seemed right that she had to move
while he, staying, flaunted the younger woman
at local meetings of the horticultural society.
The snow has begun to squall, bursts of wind
like the gusts of censure we indulge in
to gloss over our own moral lapses, to vent
our dismay at larger injustices. I envy
snow's power to cover, to wrap everything
in white cerements, to emanate virgin purity.
The wrought-iron bench in our back garden,
now a plush upholstered chesterfield. In a flurry
of back-pedalling wings, two blackcap chickadees
alight, sink into cushions. Preen.

ON THE ROAD TO COLLINGWOOD
(December 2002)

Pink, cherub-cheeked clouds
featherdust a Fra Angelico sky. Flashes
of fields between rows of leafless trees
like glimpses of an altar boy's surplice.
Lulled by the scene's prelapsarian
innocence, I sink into the passenger seat,
and leave to others the reading of road maps.

Then a false turn left into the path
of a descending car. Its speed
and the slick and steep of the slope
miscalculated. You saw it,
rear-mirrored, come at us.
I didn't, even though you say
a horn honked before
the thudding crack of steel
smacked into steel,
sheet metal crumpled.

Not the rolling over three times
to land cushioned by snow,
in the Christmas tale the hotel clerk
receives us with, all the presents
flying free of their wrappings
except the fine French wine
chosen for parents and the rum cake
in its box, unharmed. The young men

from the other car stand,
shuddering, in the pitchfork wind,
frightened they'll be found at fault,
relieved when the crash is chalked up
to the state of the road, snow swirling
across the highway in bloated clouds.

I should have confessed to the officers
where the real blame lay, named
the complacent rider: her failure
to read the signs, to recognize the angel
of near death whirling over the asphalt
in sheer organdy, obscuring a surface
already black-iced with fears.

COLLINGWOOD'S CRANBERRY INN SPA IN DECEMBER

I lie masked, swaddled, islanded
in a darkened room; voices
like the lapping of water reach in
and recede. The masseuse
is reading a message she received
on the back of a crayon drawing
of sun, butterflies and flowers in bloom.

> *Dear Carol,*
> *I want to give you a pict-*
> *ure of summer because*
> *my mom is still getting*
> *the hang of winter.*

Logy within my detox cocoon,
I feel an affinity with the mother
who hasn't yet grasped the unique
drape and flounce of winter,
may be wary of its shaky relation
to edges, distinctions, its easy collapse
of the vertical into horizontal vastness.

Winter is what I've entered.
And to be wrapped for an hour
in its antithesis is a flimsy stopgap, no
lasting defence against the season's uncharted
coordinates, its too clear
destination.

IV

After the Flower Show

Like a foxhound loosed on the hunt,
all afternoon she bounded from exhibit
to exhibit, bending, sniffing, gathering
names for a garden. *Sweet Woodruff,*
Chocolate Ruffles, Globe Blue Spruce.
Now, back home, chopping carrots
and coriander in her kitchen, she hears
a radio voice threaten shock and awe.
Trembling Aspen, Alocasia. A barrage
of Tomahawk missiles and bunker busters
thundering down. *Mountain Fire.*
The hollow premise *Halcyon Hosta*:
it'll all be over *Dark Star Coleus*
in a roar, a flash. But afterwards,

in the aftermath of the aftershock,
after sands shroud the gouges tanks
chewed in roads, after victors, drunk
on imperium, lounge in the defeated leader's
gilded palaces, after smoke ceases to plume
from the ruins of Basra, Karbala, Kirkuk:
for the truck-borne women and children
shot dead at a checkpoint, for the shrapnel-
scarred, the toddler amputees, what
sweet thereafter on the banks of the Tigris?

SPRING'S REPRIEVE

Redbud, red bird, red
diamond on a black bird's wing,
life is returning

to Kansas. Hank and Jake, sons
of part-time workers at Iola's Wal★Mart,
returned home last week from their third

tour of duty in Iraq. Turned, the earth
stirs to its seeding. And last night
the farm hunkered unharmed

for hours between cloud banks—
colossal blackboards lacerated
by lightning. This morning children

swoop, pastel-fledged,
across a gleaming lawn,
abruptly change direction, turning

and banking in unison, spread arms
dangling baskets, voices a menagerie
of chirrs and whoops. In the distance,

where lawn meets field—cliché and
schmaltz come to life—a nonchalant
cottontail munches. Then head

raised, ears alert, he hops,
rump up, under the lilac. Though
no need, given today's the one day

farmers don't bloody their hands
with rabbits, a reprieve less
random than ours last night

sandwiched untouched between lit-up
boom boxes. They call *Cercis canadensis*
redbud, but it blossoms mauve.

Gratitude is a practice, Anna e-mailed me,
Anna, whose meds keep depression at bay.
She would be grateful for such flowers and is
for waking each morning able to see, hear,
taste (this bouquet has no scent).

Among the psalms, one finds out-
pourings of thanks. But not in the Lord's Prayer,
that litany of pleas and praise to the Almighty.
And nothing wrings from the European blackbird
those virtuoso arias from atop trees and hydro poles
but competition for a mate.

I mouth "practise" and think
piano scales, Latin declensions, German irregular verbs.
Or Yoga, Pilates, workouts with weights. Can one hire
a tutor or a private trainer to come to the house?
Or must one exercise alone?

Would it be like learning
self-control, a craft, in-line skating?
Or the Buddhists' art of non-attachment?
My friend Thelma tosses at least one possession
every day.

Would practising out loud help?

The farmer, asked to repeat the name,
writes it on paper he wraps the *Crocosmia* in. I search
for a mnemonic: Cro-Magnon, maybe. Or Croatia/Bosnia.
Crows from outer space. Something cosmic. Meteoric orange,
the blossoms are, but orchid-like in their delicate and erotic taper.

FOUR TRUMPETS

An armadillo! she gasps,
tearing off the wrapping and peering in,
the faces of her friends clouding.
I love armadillos, she declares,
as the looks darken
and she falters.

The blooms are red trumpets of brushed
suede on a tall stalk, the pot
diapered in crumpled red foil. No,
not an armadillo, and she rifles
her brain ... *armature, Armageddon,
armistice*. How close
war is to peace.

Returning home she counts the stairs, *one*
to *thirty-seven*, far short of ninety-two,
the number of steps to the top
of the pyramid at Chichen Itza, with
the sacred sinkhole where Mayans sacrificed
virgins and not, as would be sensible,
villagers past their prime:
     amerind, amethyst, amorous,

the amaranths that earlier adorned
her dining room table bled dry
months ago. Where they stood she now sets
her birthday gift, a quartet
of velvet-robed Gabriels, bugles
raised to announce
  or
the trumpeter of Kracow
sounding his warning from all four
windows of the church tower at once
  or
an air raid siren's halo of flared speakers
blaring north, south, east and west:
       prepare,
   now begins another year, prepare
   amaranth, amethyst, and yes

amaryllis

THOUGH NOT ASKED

Erasmus, the earnest student of theology
urges a friend as they ride the subway
to St. Mike's. *Don't forget Erasmus.*
I want to answer, *I haven't forgotten,*
though I can only remember
fragments. Like the word "irenic." Opposite
of irascible. Erasmus, an ecumenical man
in a time of deadly dispute, his eyes and ears
honed for folly, both others' and his own.

Was it folly to begin writing poems
when already growing old? Poetry is written,
I've been told, out of new experience. Well, ageing
is new, goddamit. The newness of skin
falling in folds like a stranger's clothes. The throes
of windedness climbing subway stairs. And then
looked at no longer with desire, the new
invisibility. It would be Erasmian

to make peace with the dissonance,
the mishmash, the holy mess of life. Instead
I'm like a mirror held up to the larger
mayhem, unable to live in anything
but clutter, the chaos of books, files,
papers strewn over scuffed floors. If only

I were old-fashioned, like the excellent women
in Barbara Pym novels, resigned
to spend their days serving tea
to the locale curate, hoping to restore
order to the world by arranging
jumble sales or straightening a drawer
of handkerchiefs.

LABYRINTH

The pilgrim is invited to trace
a circuitous track that circles forward
to circle back before proceeding
toward the hub. A switchback path,
commonly box-hedged, at St. Michael's
edged with prairie stones laid out
in an ancient design—Egyptian,
Hindu, Hopi, or Cretan. At the core,

no flesh-devouring Minotaur,
only a large, blackened, debris-
strewn rock, encircled by rebuses:
pink comb, mosquito repellent,
Macdonald's coupon book, loot
from pilgrims who walked to the centre
and laid their burden down.

No token adequate
for the tangled bond with my brother,
labyrinthed through years of charge,
counter-charge, words misheard
and gestures misconstrued, maze
become Minotaur. Nor have I found

the Theseus who could cut through
our snarled skein, slay
the monster. Now, at wit's end,
if only I could lay my hands
on a sign commensurate.
If I could lift the weight of it.

I look toward the centre.

GUILTY PLEASURE

Monstrous, she fears, to feel so Candide-
contented, but spring has arrived,
and the garden returning to life

advertises for a gardener: clear away
winter's decay, fill, with impatiens,
the gaps between perennials. She cultivates

a sense of guilty pleasure, reading,
on rest breaks, Reeder's life of Akhmatova,
shunned, silenced, starved under Stalin's tyranny.

So many plants to be planted: cryptotaenia,
coriander, tilt-a-whirl coleus—names
to be chanted over the soil and mixed

with the starter fertilizer and pagan prayer
for rain and sun and, dare she ask,
while elsewhere lives are ending, green

splendour reaching to the end of summer.

SPIRÆA

Like spume on a surfer's high breaking wave
or tiers of ruffled white tulle on a 50s prom dress.
But no. Such figures merely gloss the spiræa,
in bloom every spring, serried to hedge the garden
from the street. Like a line of young girls
walking on tiptoe to their first communion then
bending to brush the earth with lace-gloved fingers.
There—and you couldn't have missed it—another
mistaken take, for spiræa is, simply, itself,
a blossoming shrub, and that should suffice. And yet
this penchant for analog—an effect, not
of the seen but of its being seen. And by whom. For some,
a lustful stirring. Yes, lustful—to encounter jets
of miniature white antimacassars gushing in faux parabolas.

WOMAN WITH WILD FLOWERS
(Odilon Redon, 1890s)

I fix my eye on her. Try to catch
her eye, but she won't return
my gaze. She has Natalie's

almond eyes, Simona's oval face,
her own look. Across the bottom
of the canvas a band of Mother-

of-God blue. In an unseen hand
a clutch of flowers
wild from a meadow. Lips

thin but not pursed, the woman stares
at nothing as though unseeing
or witnessing an inner

clair-obscur.   I stand
and stand before it. Time
at a standstill. She sees.

Sees. Behind her,
deepening and spreading, a splotch
of intense yellow.

LEAFING OUT

Outside my window, Aspen
in an ecstasy of photosynthesis:
leaves in the early stages of unfurling
breathe in sunlight,
exhale it back to me,
transmuted into a fresh green, a callow green,
a green so new it still contains
the yellow of the sun.

BLUEING BLUE

The way to the Chagall windows is a via dolorosa through displays
of halberds and poleaxes, awl-pikes and a particularly wicked instrument
called a military fork. I follow the directions straightahead, marching by much

armour, many rapiers, a walking-stick axe with pistol and blade,
a thrusting sword, parrying dagger, crossbows, and matchlock muskets.
The latter with enamel inlaid handles and barrels. The ornamental embedded

in the murderous. Indigo, cornflower, cerulean, midnight. School-children,
trooped past where I sit agape at the floor-to-ceiling glass, receive no command
to right face and gaze at *der-blaue-Engel*, Minerva-at-dusk, Cabinet-of-Dr.-Caligari

blue, a saturated tunnelling, cockeyed curving, buckling, swirling,
arcing blue. This is blue streak-, bolt from out of-, intoxicating blue. Not blue note
or blue stocking or blue funk blue. A couple ask a man to take a snapshot

of them entwined before the triptych. Seen from across the courtyard,
the blue-stained windows reflect tree and sky like other windows viewed
from outside, except this glass is webbed with lead, looped and swung,

triangulated. Later, the sun cloud-shrouded, the blues deepen, darken,
brightening a yellow orb, a candlestick, an ecstatic dancer falling
through space, a human torso breaking out into leaf. Everything

celebratory: three violins, light on an open book, the six-pointed star
radiating not an iceberg- or bloody murder- but a true blueing
blue.

A THIN BLUE LINE
(After Elaine Whittaker's installation "Miasma")

Respiratory masks, the blue of a glacial lake,
Saskatchewan sky. Capricious
the divide between exquisite
and miasmic. Cupped to cover mouth and nose,
illuminated like miniature Chagall windows,
Chinese lanterns, they hang in staggered rows,
their elastic bands looped over nails. What beauty
resides in microbial menace—viruses, bacteria,
fungi, protozoa. They shudder
in the fan-stirred air. TB's squadron
of red winged dragons. Creutzfeldt-Jakob's
apple blossoms in a lavender sky, gonorrhea's
purple berries bubbling up from a mauve bath.
All successful in their leap, their Übersprung,
water and air the obliging conductors.
German measles' cheese and zucchini pizzas,
tetanus' indigo footprints, syphilus' electric
blue eels. Fortunate the ten noblemen and women
who, escaping a Florence ravaged by Black Death,
decamped into the Tuscan hills and survived,
passing the time telling tales. A friend
visiting the show remembers the artist
a schoolgirl turning somersaults in gym,
and they're all turning fifty now. As yet unscathed
by bubonic plague—ashes, ashes, all fall down—
or any of the other predators decorating
the white gallery walls—hemorrhagic fever, rabies,
cholera, meningitis. An aquarium of tropical fish—
malaria, encephalitis, SARS. A garden of exotic
flowering plants—Chlamydia, leukemia, leprosy,
HIV-AIDS. A Tiffany's showcase of precious
and semi-precious stones—anthrax, gangrene,
cowpox—polished and glowing. A thin blue line.

CONSTANT

As a girl, she drew close to the mountains,
their silent thereness, whether visible to the eye

or veiled. Grew partial to their reclusive habits,
emulated their long withdrawals behind haze

or clotted cloud, retiring to her room for days.
And when the sky turned that monotone grey, dropping

low and sliding along the horizon like liquid ash,
she sensed their presence, their unseen mass

steadying as the Nicene Creed. Grown older,
she has returned to live at their feet and see them rise,

on camas-blue mornings, lofty, the air sweet
from the garden she tends the way she might have tended

a lover had she found one as constant as a Garry Oak Meadow
with shooting star, erythronium, laurel-leaved Daphne.

UNBALANCE

Adrift as a balloon let slip
from a child's grasp, my path
erratic as a June bug's bumping,
light-blinded, into walls,
I've come unstuck with age, lost
purchase. Been cut loose. Converse

of the game we children,
costumed in summer twilight,
played aeons ago on a sprawling lawn,
one child spinning another
until the earth, tipsy on its axis, tilted
from the sun, slipping off ellipse
into happy aimlessness. Let go and thrown

for a loop, we froze in mid-
pirouette or on grass-soiled knees,
askew arms stiffened to stone. Moments
later, dizziness spent, we reversed
our metamorphosis and sprang back
into movement, the world an out-of-kilter
carousel, rising and falling in ever
loopier circles as we spun and spun,

mainlining vertigo but still
clutching the cord
to a core.

LATE APRIL IN VENEZIA

Asparagi bianci—bundles of it
for sale on campos and along the canals.
Fresh white asparagus. But none to eat
in trattoria or bar. Sharing a meal
of this seasonal delicacy might heal our rift
as strips of metal brace crumbling brick facades.
        Earlier, in the church of Santa Lucia,
we saw a woman, black-shawled,
light a candle to the patroness of sight
often portrayed serving two eyeballs
on a platter like stuffed olives. One could see
her mortal remains inside a glass casket—
desiccated feet, face masked in silver. A body
free of corruption—sweet-smelling sign
of sanctity.
        So many saints preserved—in whole
or in part: St. Catherine's thumb, St. Dominic's
fibula. *Saints preserve us!* my mother would exclaim
whenever faced with the untoward.
        And this despite her Protestant faith's
centuries-old disposal of all saints,
as idolatrous trash. Hair, bones, raiment—
anything in the way of relic received
no decent burial, their power of solace,
scorned.
        Some years ago, in Köln,
I lit a candle to Saint Anthony, restorer
of lost objects. Today I wonder if he
might also restore lost affection, lost
love, and wish we could make a pilgrimage
to Padua, to the basilica of San Antonio
where his uncorrupted body lies
entombed.
        I stand breathing in the incense
of the wisteria hanging over Venice's bulkheads
like voluptuous clusters of tangy, ripe grapes
as you light with your eyes
the creamy-white candles of the Castanea.

EINE RUHE

Eine Ruhe. Fast wie Morandi.
That's what she seeks. Not death's
rest in peace, but an inner calm.
Almost like Morandi. His vases, jugs,
bowls painted again and again with just
enough variation. And no ghostly
emptiness. Especially not emptiness.
Instead to wake to a sudden summer rain,
almost tropical, and to lie in bed listening,
without thought, wholly immersed
in the rush of sound. Or to gaze at a clay pot,
hand-turned, a bit wonky, standing by itself
on a window sill, the shadow cast in the present
schon vom Vergangenen ergriffen, already
overtaken by shadows from the past.

DOING

What to live for, if not
to do? Everybody does.
As in the old song,
even the birds.

But I don't mean
falling in love. No, I'm talking about
labour. *Homo faber.* Meaning-
ful busyness. Even the *vita*

contemplativa is a doing
of sorts, like mulling over,
wool-gathering. However still
the body. And meditation,

cousin to emptying, gleaning,
draining—pail of water,
harvested field, wound.
And remembering, thinking

back. Not merely lively,
but constructive. Look
how we amend and
recast our pasts. Tear

down and reconstruct
the parental home. Stealthily
I move the young girl's bedroom
to the end of the second-storey hall,

open the windows to sunlight
burning through mist off Phinney Bay.
Form a half circle of diminutive chairs,
plop onto each a Raggedy Ann

or Andy, teddy bear, Dumbo,
or ringlet-crowned china doll.
Their eyes, ball-and-socketed glass
or cross-stitched stars of thick black thread,

attend, more acutely than anyone
ever will again, to the child
at the blackboard easel, chalk in hand,
writing words and more words.

unser schwarzer Tag—our black day

Mahlzeit—literally "mealtime," a standard mid-day meal greeting
Vati—dad
Ein Rätzel—a puzzle
die Spuren—the traces
echt Nürnberg Lebkuchen—genuine Nuremberg gingerbread

der Erde gleich gemacht—razed to the ground
Wehrmacht—Armed Forces of Germany during World War II

Kunstverein—art institute

Umbenennung—renaming
Umwälzung—revolution
Straße—street
Leibstandarte—body guard
Bundesarchiv—Federal Archives
Stolpersteine—cobblestones designed to be tripped over
Neue Nationale Galerie—New National Gallery

Übersprung—leap

Eine Ruhe. Fast wie Morandi.—A rest, stillness. Almost like Morandi.
schon vom Vergangenen ergriffen—already overcome by what has passed
(these lines from Ulla Hahn's novel *Unscharfe Bilder* [Blurred Pictures], 2003)

NOTES

The Jack Gilbert quotation is from *Refusing Heaven* (Alfred A. Knopf, 2005), p. 65.

The Anne Compton quotation is from *processional* (Fitzhenry & Whiteside, 2005), p. 28.

DEDICATIONS

"Memory Work" is for Peter Harris, "Soda Pop Sisters of the Sock Hop" for the girls of Queen Anne High School, "Glass Equus: Elegy" for Jeannie Lespérance, "At the Chinese Cemetery" for Alison and Jim Prentice, "Backlog" and "Hand-me-downs" for Dwight and Robert Boyd, "On the Road to Collingwood" for Narda Razack, "Spring's Reprieve" for Emily and Clara Boyd, "Crocosmia" for Anna Quon, "Four Trumpets" for Maureen Hynes, and "Constant" for Sylvia Van Kirk.

ACKNOWLEDGEMENTS

To Dwight Raymond Boyd, my deep gratitude for believing in me, and to John Buschek, for believing in this book.

Thanks also to the editors of the following journals where a number of these poems, often in a slightly different form, first appeared: *ARC, Atlantis: A Women's Studies Journal, Event, The Fiddlehead, The Malahat Review, MIX Magazine, Pagitica, Queen's Feminist Review, Quills*, and *Word: Toronto's Literary Calendar.*

Aide-mémoire would not have been possible without the encouragement, support, inspiration and constructive criticism I have been fortunate enough to receive from a host of people including: Kelley Aiken, Marilyn Bowering, Marlene Cookshaw, Stan Dragland, Rebecca Fredrickson, Peter Gizzi, Louise Halve, Donna Kane, Don McKay, A.F. Moritz, Molly Peacock, Elizabeth Philips, Norma Rowen, Rhea Tregebov, Gerry Shikatani, Sheila Stewart, and the faithful members of my poetry group—Sue Chenette, Maureen Harris, Patria Rivera, and Julie Roorda.

I should also like to express my appreciation to the Banff Centre's 2003 Wired Writing and 2005 Writing Studio programmes, the 2004 Sage Hill Fall Poetry Colloquium, the 2006 St. Petersburg Summer Literary Seminars, and an October 2006 Ragdale Foundation Residency.

About the Author

Author of *They're Still Women After All: The Second World War and Canadian Womanhood* (McClelland & Stewart 1986) among other academic studies, Ruth Roach Pierson published her first book of poems, *Where No Window Was*, with BuschekBooks of Ottawa in the spring of 2002, a year after retiring from thirty-one years of teaching as historian and feminist scholar first at Memorial University of Newfoundland and later at the Ontario Institute for Studies in Education of the University of Toronto. Her poems have appeared in *ARC, Event, The Fiddlehead, The Literary Review of Canada, The Malahat Review, MIX Magazine, Pagitica, Pottersfield Portfolio, Prism International, Queen's Feminist Review, Quills,* and *Room of One's Own* as well as a number of anthologies. She won first place in the Third Annual Poetry contest (2002) of *Word: Toronto's Literary Calendar*, was a finalist in the poetry category of the 2003 *Pagitica Literary Contest*; and received an honourable mention in *Fiddlehead's* 2003/2004 Ralph Gustafson Contest for Best Poem. She lives in Toronto with her partner and their two cats, Haiku and Orange Roughy. *Aide-mémoire* is her second book of poems.